Her Inner Verse

fragments, feelings & freeflow

Francine Louise

Her Inner Verse (fragments, feelings & freeflow) © 2023 Francine Louise

All rights reserved.

No part of this publication may be reproduced, stored in a retrieval system, or transmitted, in any form or by any means, electronic, mechanical, photocopying, recording or otherwise, without the prior written permission of the presenters.

Francine Louise asserts the moral right to be identified as author of this work.

Presentation by *BookLeaf Publishing*

Web: www.bookleafpub.com

E-mail: info@bookleafpub.com

ISBN: 9789357441292

First edition 2023

This book was birthed & submitted on 31st January the same date as Charmian James' birthday.

Thank you for the synchronicity and subtle support from beyond the ether.

ACKNOWLEDGEMENT

My healing journey has been a very long and weavy road and I still have a fair way to go. I deeply treasure the support that I have received along the way. So to all those who have truly helped and supported me (I believe you know who you are) my heart is eternally yours.

Furthermore, I wish to recognise the support, inspiration & healing offerings of these glorious souls:

My gratitudes to Phillipa Noronha a wonderfully warm and enthused Pleasure Coach. Who awakened my soul to a kaleidoscope of joy, self love & sweetness. The experience gave my life new meaning & new creative approaches to healing.
♡

phillipanoronha.com

Honouring my dear friend Kirstine Weaver for her trauma informed Sexological Bodywork. There magic and safe space holding helped me to fearlessly find words to my internal landscape, to warmly acknowledge my

neuro-spicy and awaken to my sensual & sexually healing self.
♡
linktr.ee/Kirstine.Weaver

My love and thanks to the Messy heart ladies for feminine frolics & poetic prompts. Also to everyone who attended, witnessed & offered support at the weekly online Lovely Gatherings. Thank you Jamie Catto for bringing humanness together, in all its many shades and for offering a lifeline for consistant chilled connectedness.
♡
jamiecatto.com

My eternal love for Suzy Sunbeam who truly saw me and to June Chase for endless enthusiasm & encouragement. Special thanks to Vicki Moore for last minute proof reading and for being a longstanding sources of light, laughter & sanity in my life. Huge gratitudes to my parents for all they have supported me through, and to my son, my sunshine, my greatest teacher and greatest love. For him I have persevered, grown & overcome.

Finally, thank you to Vanessa Potter at Parkbathe for inviting me to deepen my connection with nature.
♡
linktr.ee/parkbathe

Thank you for having and reading this book. I am hugely grateful for the opportunity from BookLeaf Publishings and Sonia. The experience of gathering my poetry for print has chiselled beautifully outside of my comfort zone and offered interesting new learning about myself. The process of working to a deadline has been particularly daunting. Also to think, write or edit poetry under stress; a near impossible challenge. Being aware of myself as dyslexic and a perfectionist l have so often avoided putting myself 'out there'. In bringing this book to fruition and stepping out of my own way, it is wholey a breakthrough. So regardless of typos and tweeks that remain, this book offers a reminder of the ongoing creative process, that never ends, and is a celebration of freedom; when one departs from paralysing perfectionism. I truly hope that you, the reader of this book will feel encouraged and inspired for your own personal journey of expression, creativity and expansion, in following your hearts calling. From my heart to yours ♡

PREFACE

Glimmers of wisdom that come through my poetry hint towards a more deeply spiritually evolved version of myself that in truth l am yet to become. I am still very much in a process of pondering and integrating. I am still gettng to know myself as a poet and spokenword artist. It remains an exciting learning process.

In recent years l have re-connected more deeply with nature, and simultaneously l found a greater freedom of linguistic expression. Nature and poetry became an interwoven aspect of selfcare for me, and l believe has assisted me in experiencing a more harmonious connection to myself. I now also treasure my connection with the flow of universal creative energy and believe the combination of nature, creativity and emotional expression to be a powerfully healing combination.

I would like to take this opportunity to thank you, for having and reading this little book. I am hugely grateful for the opportunity from BookLeaf Publishings and to Sonia [Surname] for her kindness, patience and attention to detail. The experience of gathering my poetry together for print, truly chiselled beautifully outside of my comfort zone and offered interesting new learning about myself. The process of working to a deadline has been particularly daunting. Similarly to think, write or edit poetry under stress; a near impossible challenge.

Being aware of myself as dyslexic and a perfectionist I have so often avoided putting myself 'out there'. In bringing this book to fruition and stepping out of my own way, it represents a beautiful breakthrough. So I hope, regardless of typos and tweeks that remain, this book is a reminder of the ongoing creative process, that never ends, and is a celebration of freedom; when one departs from paralysing perfectionism. I truly hope that you, the reader of this book will feel encouraged & inspired for your own personal journey of expression, creativity & expansion, in following your hearts calling. From my heart to yours ♡

Remember

Is it now time to crawl out

Of my January shell?

Or to wait out, the Winter

Forgotten

I'm hidden so well

To curl into darkness

Surrender to the deep

Or to battle internal forces

And try to swim free

Unsure of the road now

I've fallen far from the path

But they say the road that's less traveled

Is the true journey of the heart.

~

And the rain can wash away

The most poignant pain of the past

To dissolve the hardened sediment

That has congealed around our hearts.

And we can return to flesh and life

And try our best to always remember

That our bodies are intricately weaved

And a sacred expression of nature.

Share my Soul

If I share my soul with you,

It is not I, who seeks approval,

For to share myself, with a love of self,

As flowers, flower purely for their own renewal.

And I truly try not to question nature with the mind,

I believe it seeks only our truest soul connection,

For us to own ourselves, independent from brain and advancing interference,

And to ground down in our humanity to shine as a true reflection.

Inertia. Dark night.

There is no light within

My chest an empty crag of rock forgot

Claws for ribs

Remnants of the jagged beast

His talons left behind

In place

Of

My once

Pounding flesh

My beating heart

My happiness?

I tell myself at each new day

To be more loving

Kind to self

I will return You will survive

I am still human You are still alive

But each and every day

I slowly turn away

Recoil from kindness

Rebuff my own sweet care

Freeze up

Burn out

Deplete

And now

Though l begin to heal

And excavate the remnant parts

Yet still I cease to be....

And Now?

Smile, stay quiet and pretend you're ok

You lead, I will follow and give my power away

But not today.

The sludge evaporates

The night turns day

May this treacle hostility

Melt and be swept far away.

I will not cower

Or turn my face in shame

We are both deeply wounded

Let us not place blame.

But the dots don't join up, in the way that you think

I will not be tarnished, shamed or pushed to the brink

I've been there before

And I broke

That fragile thread

The patterns you're sewing are now just in your head

I will plough through this mud

With momentum and grace

You want to bring hatred

Well let us stand face to face

And you will see

I have freed me

You're hold on me; gone

There is no, on and on

I forgive you

I free you

I thank you

And now?

I've moved on.

Spirals

Emotion spiraled

                in my heart today

She rose in wisps and waves

      In breath ~

          ~

          ~

          ~

       Ggggurgling

                in my throat

    Spilling forth

           From clouded eyes

Words

    streamed

        down

              my

                    face.

Retrieved

I love myself enough now

To finally let you go

To have felt what I have felt

And now I truly know

It wasn't all about you

Or for you to love me back

You have your own learning pathway

And I feel your hardships stacked

But in the act of loving

And opening my heart

I miraculously

Healed aspects of myself once froze apart.

The melting easing and reviving

Of cells thought nearly dead

Awakening hope and courage

It flicked a light bulb in my head

To see myself more clearly

Outdated patterns

Perfect flares

My attachments fears and traumas

To no longer be ignored.

And rejection was the gift

To return me to myself

To return me to those splintered parts

That needed no one else

But for me to do the welding

Reinforcing and the work there

To dig a little deeper

To see what truly lurked there

I uncovered knots of pain and hurt there

And a gradient of fear to be unlovable

Which caused me great panic and despair

But to feel and heal and deal with all the aspects now laid bare.

And this feeling isn't heartbreak

In fact its heart awake

An intense reboot

Resilience build

Though bitter sweet for my own sake

And now I nourish and rebuild myself from a deeper place within

To be my one true best of friend

To heal the outer ~ inner din.

And l realise it's not about keeping busy

New distractions, getting out there

For me it's about true reverence

Self acceptance

And the deepest sacred selfcare.

Flames

I read somewhere that the fires of suffering become the light of consciousness.

But it is not for us to choose, accept or welcome suffering.

And not to strive harshly, endlessly or self sabotage for consciousness.

But to dance with life,

Dance with the flames.

To respect and acknowledge the scorching timber,

But not to become it.

Be grounded, so not to fan the flames.

Yet light in our humanness,

For underneath we all contain scorched earth.

So may we hold the rains of compassion,

And journey gently forth.

While the fires rage intensely.

Yet flicker by flicker,

A warmth, a light,

To guide us yet,

To less smoke filled skies.

When the crows sing from within

What if you cut me open

And all your crows and blackbirds were set free

Flying from my body

And you'd be there to see

Precisely the true impact

Of all you took from me

To realise, understand, acknowledge

That only after,

An empty shell

Was ever left of me.

Rose Worship

To journey within the pentagram of Venus.

Deep down within the Rose.

To follow the ancient wisdom of feminine teachings,

For Maya Luna knows

Praise be the Goddess.

Praise be, for our own hearts,

To cultivate a truer hope, beyond illusion,

From deep inside the dark.

To water the seeds of compassion

And be a wash with sweet kindness to self,

To accept here. Now.

As exactly where we are.

No more distraction or body else.

A place to feel it all,

No fixing, doing or denial.

Where the soul may rest.

And fill with blessed relief,

To truly acknowledge our impermanence,

and our human core of grief.

To face ourselves,

Within the Rose.

Our beauty is not without the thorn.

But to bloom with gratitude

For the fragility of life,

And cultivate our own darkness,

Yes, die and be reborn.

Lets revive the truth of feminine wisdom,

To be soft, sense-you-all and seasonal

Is a gift and our true power

So may we stand a little taller and rooted now,

With our sisters,

And commune with this holy flower.

Heart Howl

The moon and I, are kin,

and I can declare my love outlandishly,

I'm yours, pearly white magnificence.

Spherical illumination of my inner dreams,

So beautiful and watery,

Your teary eye now watching over me.

For the moon and I, are kin,

And I can share my secrets there-in.

Create my alter,

Lovingly as if my daughter.

Spread arms like wings,

And howl to my fullness,

My sweetly pain release

To ease me into dream filled sleep,

Until a new cycle and we repeat..

The new moon and I, are kin,

With full mother moon and father son.

To know my true self and fear no one.

To unburden my heart,

And live from its centre.

This magnetic pull returns

Towards a new healing encounter.

The hug of health.

The safety of skin on skin

Loving moon, my friend,

I must sew my own heart,

And sew myself

With such love, once again.

Mermaid story

A mermaid once, was lost at sea

And miraculously she came ashore to visit me

She spoke with heart of her sad soul

Her endless quest to feel fulfilled and whole

She'd journeyed to the greatest depths

Travelled the world; it's length and breadth

She shared her sorrows, her sea of tears

Hopes now shipwrecked, that revealed remnant fears

She told me, she'd been searching for a forgotten key

And for the truths of the universe I found her asking me....

I told her plain and honestly

"I know little of feeling or ever being so free

But the searching, it never ever stops

The searching and hoping never stops

It continues onwards and deep within

The search for ever greater meaning

There is no key or door that will reveal

The key is to deeply trust, in how you truly feel

To have embodied presence offers inner knowing

Not what our programming mind is relentlessly showing"

All at once the mermaid with a splash was no more

And I found myself again alone upon the shore

Feeling revived and elated but wholly unsure

Had it been magic, a figment, or perhaps nothing at all?

But many years later

I felt strongly called to return

To that very same place

And as I daydreamed

Looking out to sea

I saw a familiar face

And she was not alone,

A unicorn, he reared his head

Sweet fairies of the coral, conjured mischief unsaid

A dragon exhaled fire in a fierce feminine dance

And a gentle giant stomped despairingly to witness all of humanity's intolerance

And the beautiful mermaid, she smiled at me

Her arms both raised, waving gratefully

For she had found at last her loving tribe

Heartwarming company for a more fulfilling life's ride

For her true search had not been to find fellow mer-men and maids

Though they may have been similar in looks and even things that they say

But she had learnt that a true mirror is not found in broken glass

And to trust her deeper instincts and to not let those tender hearted moments pass

For reciprocated acceptance, compassion, kindness and understanding

Whisked up in a shared experience of growing care and trust expanding

For she had found her true soul warriors who had become her musketeers

To comfort, encourage and dispel all her outdated and isolating fears

Immersed in her own wisdom she had found a safe way to feel connection

To reveal and treasure once hidden aspects of herself in new differing reflections

Within herself, she had nurtured a safe home that never ends

And of course it makes everything magnificently better

As they beckoned me, when life is shared with such true friends.

Painting, pain-thing

Turning towards beauty

In the midst of grief

Though it won't take away the pain

It may stir up colours of emotion

The sting of tears released

Within a sacred brush of melancholy

It can offer bittersweet relief

~

Letting Go

I continue to shed the tears

That swallowed up my heart

But l now un-tie the loss and fears

From the threads once tangled in the dark.

I now give my delicate heart safe home

And turn my face towards the light

I now release my pain, like butterflies

So love

May dance

Flow free

Take flight.

Momentum

Closeness, now hollow

I hold my bare arms adrift

To fill my empty aura

With more sense of myself in carnate

My bleeding heart, my pulse, my beat

To dance, to shake, to feel my feet

On woodland paths, wrapped up in wool and fleece

I find my peace.

Under blanket of trees, heart warm by fireside

Pen poised to discover my deeper inner desires

Evolve

I choose to evolve and let go

Releasing from the need to justify

Apologise, excuse, lie, deny

Or even ask the question, why?

I choose to evolve and stay rooted

In deeper connection with myself, first

Delving deeper with others and the earth

Filling my own heart with rich soil, to rebirth

I now choose to evolve as 'mother' / 'giver'

While still feeding my own needy soul

To lovingly allow creativity, achievement and goal

And to love myself so deeply

To fully encapsulate myself as whole

While knowing myself

Part of the greater whole.

I choose to evolve and heal, from what's passed

And return to THIS moment as sacred

Accepting death as an inevitable part

But for all other moments, be alive

Spreading my branches

and at home in my heart

I choose to evolve, with more ease

To acknowledge the whispering glint of desire in me

Acknowledging all emotional frequencies as simply part of humanity

And see myself more clearly

The truth and depth of me

Is that

I am a tree

A uniquely beautiful tree

So l choose to evolve and dive deeper

in life's spiral interwoven with the seasons

It becomes perfectly fine to go slow

Though my pure, gentle and loving wish
remains to grow

I set my own pace, blossom at will

Bending and swaying

Shedding leaves as l go

Delicious Darkness

You were such delicious darkness

And I too was darkness, but hidden in light

An instant magnetic attraction

That felt intoxicatingly right.

Both emotionally troubled

Our wounds were still precariously fresh

Dripping and glistening intensely

Each pleading for healing

Through the connection of flesh.

I was quick to discover you were locked in pain

While l was a heady brew of pain and growth

I vowed to heal and to bring you with me

Yet found myself stuck in self sabotage

To never break this unfathomable oath.

And while you became a shadow

l tried to be your shadow's heart

To allow our love to bloom through chaos

Yet plagued with oppositional forces

To inevitably deplete and savagely set us apart.

Towards me, you became a long icy night

And l, an endless grey grueling day

We each became strangers to the other

Until there remained no hope to sustain

Our misconstrued attachment and lost love in all its ways.

Woodland Weave

I wish not to preach, but to spread my feet

Grounded now on an open, visible path

I had been stumbling so long in the wilderness

I had almost forgotten how to laugh

But now I find myself in a quiet quaint clearing

No rumbling forest threats, just yet

And I wonder if I can move forward now?

Despite my demons crouched, who refuse to forget

These precious painful parts of self

I now hold close and sweet caress

The parts that had to learn the hard way

Neglected and expected, to recover under duress.

But kindness is my better friend

And the warm wisdom of women, scares me less

But still I'm yet to fully embrace

The unknown

Untrusted

Deep dark mysteries

Of our true and sacred Goddess.

And as I more gently accept myself
My body, womb and heart
Creating ceremony and mandalas to offer her my art

I step forth on a new woodland weave

Supported by ancient whispers upon the breeze

And with softness and intention as my guiding alter
I give thanks and witness myself as the Goddesses daughter.

Response

No words come under pressure

And l wonder at the freeze

The weight of expectation

The familiar threat response

That never fails to interseed.

I see myself grinning and laughing awkwardly

Though his smarminess makes me retch

To fawn despite the distrust that creeps

Up my spine, to rear its warning head

The blind panic that over takes me

The shoes that find my feet

The afeared spirit within now bursting out

So the only way to stay whole is to flee

I breath,

Run

For perceived freedom;

Relief

I greet.

Heart vs Mind

The questions l ask myself?

Is my heart sleeping?

Surrounded by walls

A castle once for a prince and a princess

But now jaded and cold.

Is my heart frozen?

In the ice of the past

Or from fear of that virus

Now disguised under a mask.

Or is my heart just vacant?

Zoned out, no response

Can we resuscitate?

Or was it death, after loving just once.

And the heart asks,

Can I be who I truly am?

The mind says

Do I like who she is?

These are the questions

That have my heart and mind in a tiz of utter confusion.

And perhaps my heart is just fine

Fully whole, in one piece

But the communication between heart and mind

Is where the true problem is.

Because the mind will not listen

Follow or trust the heart's lead,

The heart feels that the mind is paranoid

And the mind thinks the heart's too much greed.

The heart cries, let me love.

But the mind replays mistakes of the past

Unforgiving of failure as a simple learning path

So the inner turmoil causes pain and chaos

With a boundaryless heart open wide

And a overprotective untrusting mind

That fears she'll just let half the world inside

And perhaps the heart isn't breaking

But is breaking free to be released

Of the minds power and dominance

And relieve the heart for ever more peace.

And what we now need

Is to give a little more space (Not from loving)
No

But from the mind, time apart

To trust and more deeply-listen and to champion our hearts.

Friction

I wanted to create friction

To feel the warmth of a spark

But I had to run away wildly,

Once the matches I'd been throwing

Got caught on your heart.

~

Love crept towards me

Slowly on its own

My heart no longer etched in stone

So l did not scamper, hide or retreat

But found firm ground, to be present, and plant, weary, cautious, feet

To stay and feel the feelings, be open to recover

The delicious long forgotten sense of vibing with another

To feel alivened and revived, I was soon quick to rediscover.....

That I am not as broken as I had first thought

All the pieces of my puzzle may be scrambled

But they're here and effectively re-caught

It's ok to feel and it's still safe to care

And this butterfly admiral that flutters near

Blesses me with energy and fills my heart with hope

For a new more conscious path and a more creative way to cope

And though, I know, this will only be for a temporary transitional spell

If happiness could stay with me, just for a little while.

Cloud dancing

Self worth rising?

I'm encircled by dark clouds

As we move together in a *Stratus* dance

My first fragmented thought

Was that, there was no space or time for love

Where grief weaves in, its blustering, clouding, thrust.

Yet the *Altostratus* dance ignites

A sexual energy within

To heal those molecules once filled

With shame, self loathing, and sin.

So I may *Cumulus* courage

And burn once again bright skies

For no one, but my own self healing

And my delighted *Nimbus* filled eyes.

For now tears and darkness become decadence

Grief is sweet sacred release

To sooth my soul to this hypnotic *Cirrus* beat.

Sweet nectar to connect so sensually

To my own internal trance

A deliciousness, to be my own saviour

Is my true thrilling wanderlust romance.

The waste lands

Curling in towards Winter

Our bodies plead to slow down

To feel the shedding

Yet jagged

Roughness

The exfoliation, like sand.

And when we feel that pressing raw-ness

Dry skin needs oil and our sense-you-all touch

To be there to catch and hold ourselves

When things start to feel too much.

But to allow ourselves to feel what's there

To cradle our tender heart

To grieve for our failures and losses

And for those who now've depart.

And though we may try to numb out

Real life drips between the cracks

Filling us up with unsettlement

And a need to question the narrative, perhaps?

For life lifts sandpaper to our hearts

The grate of the consumerist traps

Society digs us deeper down

In the

Divide

Between the have's, have-nots and collapse.

And amid all of the busy, striving and distraction

They don't want us to try, or fully understand.

Why

Poverty

Inequality

And sorrow flows

In the veins throughout these lands.

And we all try hard to ignore it, but

Injustice soaks, deep within us now.

Poisoning the flower-bed of our existence

And becomes a place we fear to plough.

Yet l don't advocate Winter numbing

For it's the slow tightening that intensifies the ache

Balancing precariously upon a premise

Of illusion and disillusionment

That for me is getting more difficult to shake.

We are not all meant to paint on smiles and clown

To pretend we are continuously happy

Though apparently it's ok now to not be ok.

But we are being led to journey deeper within

To meet ourselves more plain.

To feel the disparity and discontentment

To let it cut us deep

So we may grieve in the well of our humanness

And begin

With small steps

And for some of us, brave the leap.

To catapult our hearts into compassion

And shower kindness where we can

This life is not all about the money and superficial

Beneath there is a more rooted and wondrous plan.

But first we must no longer fear to face

The darker uncomfortable truths

Of the negative agenda that's in action

And our false sense of security

We fear to lose.

And must we lose our ego's too?

Perhaps no...

For our ego is simple our wounded parts

That need more witnessing and love

It's not about transcending our humanity

Or to depend solely on saviors outside of us, or up above.

But to truly use our discernment

To no longer believe the lies

(Even the ones we like to tell ourselves)

But trust our own inner body wisdom more

To stand united and sacred as sovereign within ourselves.

And to not fill our heart too full

With the doom and gloom that foretells

But stay open in our minds and hearts

To more loving and life nourishing realms.

Milton Keynes UK
Ingram Content Group UK Ltd.
UKHW020807080823
426520UK00017B/846